Make and Use
Masks

Anna-Marie D'Cruz

WAYLAND

First published in 2007
by Wayland

© Copyright 2007 Wayland

Wayland
338 Euston Road
London NW1 3BH

Wayland Australia
Level 17/207 Kent Street
Sydney NSW 2000

Senior Editor: Jennifer Schofield
Designer: Jason Billin
Project maker: Anna-Marie D'Cruz
Photographer: Chris Fairclough
Proofreader: Susie Brooks

Acknowledgements:
The Publishers would like to thank the following models:
Emel Augustin, Ammar Duffus, Teya Hutchison and Robin Stevens.

Picture Credits:
All photography Chris Fairclough except
page 4 top: Archivo Iconografica, S.A./CORBIS; page 4 bottom:
Reuters/CORBIS; page 5 top: José T Poblete/CORBIS; page 9
top: Dallas and John Heaton/Free Agents Limited/CORBIS

CIP data
D'Cruz, Anna-Marie
   Masks. - (Make and use)
   1. Mask making - Juvenile literature 2. Masks -
     Juvenile literature
   I. Title
   646.4'78

ISBN: 978 0 7502 5052 8

Printed in China

Wayland is a division of Hachette Children's Books.

Note to parents and teachers:
The projects in this book are designed to be made by children. However, we do recommend adult supervision at all times as the Publisher cannot be held responsible for any injury caused while making the projects.

Contents

All about masks

A mask is something that covers all or part of the face to hide it or to change its appearance. Masks have decorated faces throughout history – from Stone Age huntsmen, Egyptian mummies and Greek actors to today's modern performers.

MASKS FROM LONG AGO

Masks were used as far back as the Stone Age when huntsmen are believed to have disguised themselves as animals before stalking their prey. In Ancient Egypt, funeral masks were used to cover the face of the mummy so that the dead person's soul would recognise the person's body in the afterlife. Some of these masks have been found in Egyptian tombs, such as King Tutankhamun's mask (see right).

THEATRE COSTUMES

Actors in the Ancient Greek and Roman theatres used masks to show emotion (feeling). In the Greek theatre, all the characters were played by men, so those playing women wore masks of female characters. In the Italian comedy theatre, *commedia dell'arte*, the lively characters were portrayed with the help of silly looking masks. In Japanese Noh theatre, the actors create the characters through body movement and masks (see left). Today, television and film actors wear masks as part of the special effects that help make the characters more believable.

FESTIVALS

Masks are worn during many festivals around the world. One of the most famous of these festivals is the Venice carnival. Like the New Orleans Mardi Gras in the USA, the carnival takes place before Lent and ends on Shrove Tuesday. People at the carnival wear traditional Venetian volto masks, masks of famous characters from the *commedia dell'arte*, such as Harlequin and Pierrot or fantasy masks made especially for the carnival (see right).

GET STARTED!

In this book you can discover ways of making interesting masks from around the world. Try to use materials that you already have either at home or at school. For example, for the cardboard in these projects, the backs of used-up notepads, art pads and hardbacked envelopes are ideal. Reusing and recycling materials like this is good for the environment and it will save you money. The projects have all been made and decorated for this book but do not worry if yours look a little different – just have fun making and wearing your masks. You could have a different face for each day of the week!

Aztec skull

The Day of the Dead is an Aztec celebration that is still popular in Brazil and Mexico. The Aztecs believed that death is the beginning of a new stage of life, so the Day of the Dead is a happy time to celebrate people's lives on Earth. The skull is a popular symbol of this festival. Follow the steps to make your own skull mask.

YOU WILL NEED

cream and white card
pencil
pair of scissors
glue
coloured pencils
wool
sticking tape
hole punch
elastic cord

1 Draw the shape shown onto cream card so that it is big enough to cover your face. Cut it out.

2 Use the information in the panel on the right to draw and cut out circles for the eyes. Make them large enough for you to see through. Similarly, cut out a triangular shape for your nose.

DRAWING EYES

1. Close your eyes. Use the hand that you do not use to write to point to your eyes.
2. Move your fingers onto the mask.
3. Use a pencil to mark where your fingers are and to draw eyes.
4. Cut out the eyes.

3 Draw and cut out teeth from the white card. Glue them onto the mask to make a mouth.

4 Use coloured pencils to cross-hatch parts of the mask to decorate it.

5 For the hair, cut lengths of wool and tape them to the top of the mask at the back so that they fall over the top of the mask.

6 To wear the mask, use a hole punch to make a hole on either side of the mask. Cut a cord of elastic that fits around your head, then thread it through the holes and tie it with a knot at each hole to keep it in place. Your mask is now ready to wear.

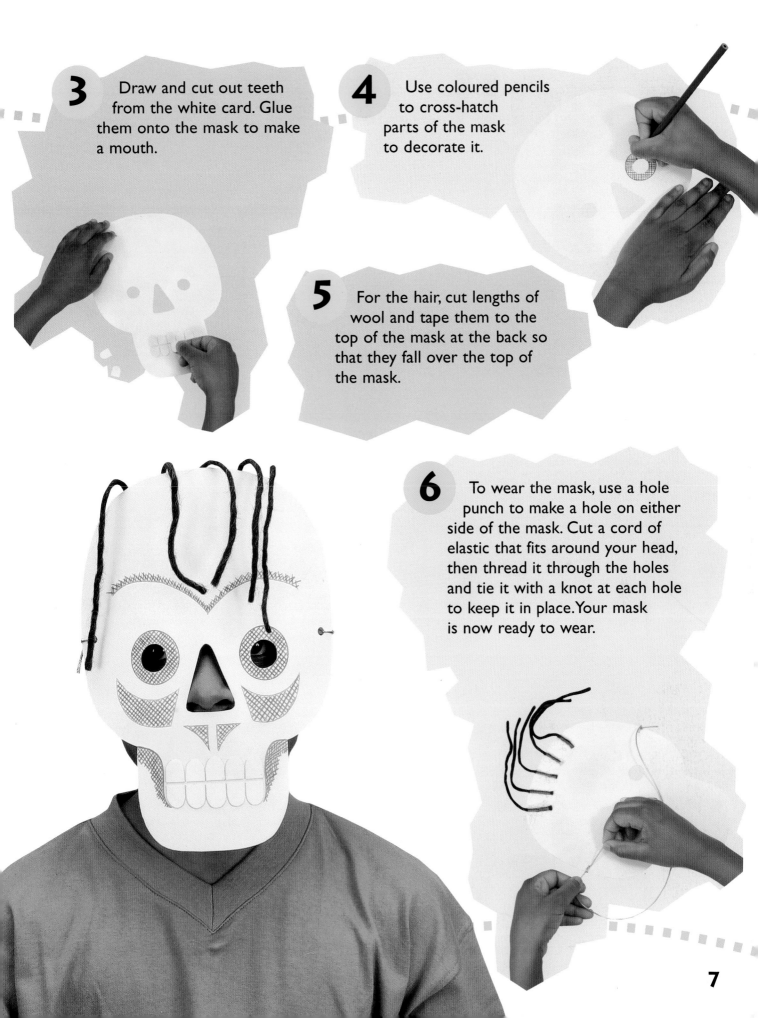

Khon mask

Khon is a style of theatre performed in Thailand where the actors wear masks or crowns to represent animals, demons and gods. The masks are brightly coloured and often have gold crowns that are decorated with jewels. Use coloured paints and lots of glitter to decorate your mask.

YOU WILL NEED

A3 sheet of coloured card
pencil
pair of scissors
newspaper
coloured paints
paintbrushes
glue
glitter
sequins
foil stars
gold pen
hole punch
elastic cord

1 Copy the shape shown onto the card, making it big enough to cover your face. Cut it out.

2 Follow the guide on page 6 to mark where the eyes need to be. Cut them out.

3 Use a pencil to draw on a design for the face.

4 Cover your work surface with newspaper. Use different coloured paints and a gold pen to decorate the face part of the mask. Leave the paint to dry.

5 To decorate the crown, cover a small section of it with glue and sprinkle it with glitter. When the glue has dried, cover the next section with glue, adding more glitter, sequins and foil stars.

KHON THEATRE

In Khon plays the actors dance and do acrobatics. They cannot do any talking because their masks cover their mouths, so instead, other actors stand to the side of the stage to sing and tell the story.

6 When the glue has dried, the mask is ready to try on. Use a hole punch to make a hole on either side of the mask. Cut a cord of elastic that fits around your head, then thread it through the holes and tie it with a knot at each side to keep it in place.

Carnival jester

Masks are made for carnivals around the world. The most famous carnivals take place in Venice, Italy, Rio de Janeiro, Brazil and New Orleans, USA. The jester is one of the most popular carnival masks. Follow the steps to make your own jester mask.

YOU WILL NEED

A3 sheet of coloured card
pencil
pair of scissors
coloured paper
glue
stapler
rik rak
ruler
double-sided tape
hole punch
elastic cord

1 Draw and cut out the shape shown from the card. Check that it fits across your face and over your nose, but does not cover your mouth. Cut out holes for your eyes, as shown on page 6.

2 Cut out shapes from the coloured paper to decorate the hat part of the mask. Staple rik rak around the edge of the eye part of the mask.

MARDI GRAS

The New Orleans Mardi Gras (which means Fat Tuesday in French), is a time of parades and masked balls. The Mardi Gras lasts for a few weeks but it ends on Shrove Tuesday – the day before Lent starts.

3 To make the nose, fold a piece of card in half. Draw a triangle onto the card that is wide enough at one end to fit onto the nose of the mask. Cut out the nose.

4 Make a small cut, about 1cm long, along the fold at the widest end of the triangle.

5 Fold each side of the small cut upwards to make tabs.

6 Put double-sided tape onto each tab to stick the nose to the mask.

7 Use a hole punch to make a hole on either side of the mask. Cut a cord of elastic that fits around your head, then thread it through the holes and tie it with a knot at each side to keep it in place. Put on the mask and get into the carnival spirit!

Bwa sun mask

Crops need rain and sunshine to grow. In many countries, people depend on the rain and sunshine for all their food. This mask is worn by people in Burkina Faso in dance ceremonies to celebrate the farming season.

YOU WILL NEED

thin corrugated cardboard
pencil
plate
pair of scissors
masking tape
newspaper
PVA glue
string
paints
paintbrushes
large lollipop stick

1 Draw around a plate onto the cardboard. Make sure the circle is large enough to cover your face. Cut it out. Use the guide on page 6 to cut out holes for the eyes.

2 To make the nose, cut a triangle of card and bend it down the middle. Put strips of masking tape down each side to stick it to the mask.

3 Spread glue around one of the eyeholes. Circle string around the eye hole until you have gone around four or five times. Do the same with the other eye hole.

12

4 To make a mouth, cut two circles from the cardboard, one smaller than the other. Glue the larger circle onto the mask where the mouth should be and then glue the smaller circle on top of that.

5 Cut triangles from the cardboard and glue them to the mask to make Sun rays. Allow all the glue to dry.

6 Cover your work surface with newspaper. Paint the mask with brightly coloured paints. When the paint is dry, tape a large lollipop stick to the bottom of the mask on the back. To wear the mask, hold it by the stick over your face.

BURKINA FASO

Burkina Faso in Africa is one of the poorest countries in the world. Farming is important to the people of Burkina Faso because most people work on farms for a living. If the crops do not grow, there will be no work or money.

Kenyan giraffe

Lots of giraffes and other animals roam the plains of Kenya in Africa. This mask is simple to make and lots of fun. When you have mastered this animal mask, why not use the template on page 15 to make a lion mask?

YOU WILL NEED

A3 sheet of yellow card
pencil
pair of scissors
orange and brown paper
glue
stapler
elastic cord

1 Copy the shape shown onto card, making sure the inner part is wide enough to cover your face. Cut out the shape. Cut out holes for the eyes, as shown on page 6.

2 Cut out shapes from the orange and brown paper. Glue them onto the mask within the inner line, so that it looks like a giraffe's face.

3 Using the template as a guide, make small cuts on the dotted lines, going up to the inner line. With the right side of the mask face down, fold up the edges. Overlap the cut edges and staple them together, but leave where the giraffe's nose meets the face unstapled.

14

4 Cut two horn shapes from the yellow card. Add a small piece of brown paper to the top of each horn and cut a fringe into it. Fold the bottom edge of each horn in by 2–3cm to staple the horn to the top of the mask.

ROARING FUN!

Use the templates below to make a lion mask.

5 Cut two ears from the card. Gently bend over the top of the ear and then the end of the ear by 2–3cm. Staple the ears to the sides of the mask.

6 Measure the elastic cord so that it can go around your head. Staple it to the sides of the mask. Your mask is now ready to wear.

Egyptian mask

In Ancient Egypt, mummies wore masks made out of wood, stone or precious metals such as gold. One of the most famous masks was worn by the Pharaoh Tutankhamun. Be a Pharaoh with your own Tutankhamun mask.

YOU WILL NEED

- paper plate – 25cm in diameter
- pair of scissors
- pencil
- 2 strips light-coloured fabric, 6cm x 22cm
- double-sided tape
- newspaper
- paints – including gold, blue and brown
- paintbrush
- card
- stapler
- large lollipop stick
- sticking tape

1 Cut off the rim of half the paper plate. Cut out holes for the eyes, as shown on page 6.

2 Use double-sided tape to stick the strips of fabric to the front of the plate, one to either side of where the rim has been trimmed off.

3 Cover your work surface with newspaper. Turn over the mask and draw a face onto the plate. Paint the plate and cloth and allow to dry.

16

4 To make a snake and vulture to decorate the mask, copy the shapes below onto card. Cut them out and paint on the details as shown. Paint the back of the vulture plain gold.

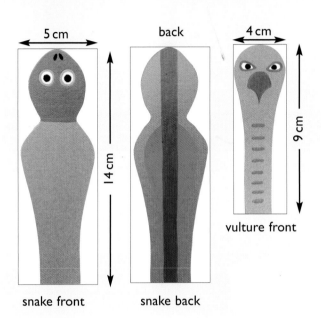

5 cm

back

4 cm

14 cm

9 cm

vulture front

snake front

snake back

5 When the paint is dry, gently bend the snake and vulture as shown, and staple them to the mask above the eyes.

6 Decorate the lollipop stick in gold and blue and when it is dry, tape it to the back of the mask at the bottom.

TUTANKHAMUN

Tutankhamun became a Pharaoh when he was about nine years old. He died before he was 20. As was the tradition, he was buried with a golden mask and many treasures. His tomb was discovered in 1922 in Egypt's Valley of the Kings, more than 3,000 years after his death. Many of the Tutankhamun's treasures can be found in museums around the world.

Greek Medusa

In Ancient Greek theatres, masks helped the actors to show sadness and happiness. They also helped the men to portray women and to be more than one person in the play. Why not wear your Medusa mask and perform in your own play?

YOU WILL NEED

card from cereal box

pencil

pair of scissors

stapler

newspaper

PVA glue

green tissue paper

paints

paintbrushes

large lollipop stick

strong tape

1 Cut the shape shown from the card. Cut holes for the eyes (see page 6) and mouth.

2 Cut snake shapes from the card. Staple them around the top of the head to look like hair.

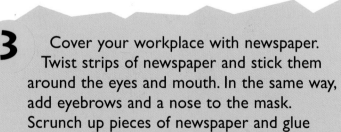

3 Cover your workplace with newspaper. Twist strips of newspaper and stick them around the eyes and mouth. In the same way, add eyebrows and a nose to the mask. Scrunch up pieces of newspaper and glue them onto the snake shapes.

4 Use glue to stick on strips of tissue paper so that the whole mask is covered.

There are many stories and myths about gods and heroes that come from the Ancient Greeks. Medusa was one of the mythological characters who had hair made of snakes. Medusa's stare would turn those people who looked at her to stone.

5 When the glue is dry, paint the eyes, eyebrows and mouth. Add eyes and mouths to the snakes, too. Leave to dry.

6 Paint the lollipop stick green. When it is dry, use strong tape to stick it to the back of the mask. Your mask is now ready to wear!

Viking mask

The Vikings were tough fighters, armed with spears, swords, axes, bows and arrows. They protected themselves with round wooden shields and helmets made of metal or leather. Make this viking mask and be a ferocious Viking warrior.

1 Blow up a balloon until it is the same size as your head. Knot the balloon. Rest the balloon on the bottom half of a shoe box.

2 Cover your work surface with newspaper. Mix a small amount of water into some glue. Use this glue mixture to stick pieces of newspaper to just over one side of the balloon. Continue until you have built up about four layers. Leave overnight to dry.

3 When the glue has dried, pop the balloon and remove it from the mask. Trim the edges of the mask. Work out where the eyes and mouth need to be and cut them out.

VIKINGS IN ENGLAND

The Vikings were mainly farmers from Denmark, Norway and Sweden. They travelled great distances in longboats to conquer and settle in other countries. In 793, the Vikings arrived in north-east England on the island of Lindisfarne, where they took over a monastery.

4 Cut strips of corrugated card and glue them onto the mask to make a cross-shaped helmet.

5 Roll up pieces of newspaper to make eyebrows, a moustache and beard. Add some tape to hold the rolls together. Glue the rolls onto the mask and allow to dry.

6 Glue on lightly scrunched pieces of kitchen foil to the top half of the mask, covering the card strips, too. Paint the face part of the mask and allow to dry.

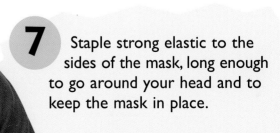

7 Staple strong elastic to the sides of the mask, long enough to go around your head and to keep the mask in place.

Glossary

acrobatics

Jumping and balancing acts to entertain people.

afterlife

Life after death. The Ancient Egyptians believed that their soul carried on living after they died.

commedia dell'arte

The Italian theatre that was popular in the sixteenth to eighteenth centuries. Many of the plays featured the same characters, for example, Pierrot the clown.

crops

Plants, such as wheat, rice and maize, that are grown for food.

cross-hatching

Shading done with small crosses.

jester

A professional clown or joker. Jesters often wore a pointy hat with bells on the end.

Lent

The time from Ash Wednesday to Holy Saturday (the day before Easter). For Christians, Lent is a time for fasting (giving up certain foods) and prayer.

masked ball

A dance where everyone wears a mask to cover some part or all of their face.

monastery

The place where monks live.

mummy

A body that has been wrapped in oils and bandages to preserve it or stop it from decaying.

myths

Traditional stories.

Pharaoh

A ruler of Ancient Egypt.

recycling

To recycle something is to change it or treat it so that it can be used again. For example, the metal in drinks cans can be recycled into other metal things.

reusing

To use something again for a different purpose.

Shrove Tuesday

The day before Ash Wednesday – the start of Lent. Because Lent is a time of fasting, people would use up their flour and eggs to make pancakes which is why people eat pancakes on Shrove Tuesday.

Stone Age

The time, thousands of years ago, when weapons and tools were made out of stone.

symbol

A mark or object that is used to represent something. For example, a skull is popular symbol for the Day of the Dead festival.

tabs

Flaps or small pieces that stick out of something.

tombs

Places where people are buried.

FURTHER INFORMATION

www.thebritishmuseum.ac.uk/whatson/touring/masks/index.html
   The website for the British Museum which has an on-line exhibition of masks.
www.venicemaskshop.com
   This on-line shop has many different masks, from traditional carnival masks to masks that resemble *commedia dell'arte* characters.
www.hamillgallery.com/SITE/MasksandHeads.html
   This gallery has loads of photographs of traditional African masks, including Bwa masks worn in Burkina Faso.
www.masksoftheworld.com
   An information-packed website with pictures of masks from around the world.
www.thaitambon.com/bk/Khonmask2_420.jpg
   Pictures of Khon masks to give you inspiration for your own mask.

Note to parents and teachers:

The website addresses (URLs) included in this book were valid at the time of going to press. However, because of the nature of the Internet, it is possible that some addresses may have changed, or sites may have changed or closed down since publication. While the author and publishers regret any inconvenience this may cause the readers, no responsibility for any such changes can be accepted by either the author or the publisher.

Index